If . . . then . . .

If . . . then . . .

ANDY B. HOOK

RESOURCE *Publications* · Eugene, Oregon

IF . . . THEN . . .

Resource Publications
An Imprint of Wipf and Stock Publishers
199 W. 8th Ave., Suite 3
Eugene, OR 97401

www.wipfandstock.com

PAPERBACK ISBN: 978-1-6667-1532-3
HARDCOVER ISBN: 978-1-6667-1533-0
EBOOK ISBN: 978-1-6667-1534-7

04/29/21

"Beauty is the first test: there is no permanent place
in the world for ugly mathematics."

—G.H. HARDY

CONTENTS

Point	3
Definitions & Dimensions	4
Postulate I	5
Postulate II	6
Postulate III	7
Postulate IV	8
Postulate V	9
5th Postulate Revisited	10
Axiom #1	11
Axioms #2 & 3	12
Axiom #4	13
Axiom #5	14
Tesselation	15
Pythagorean Triplets	16
3 Problems	17
A Famous Death	18
The Fundamental Theorem	21
Limits	22
Continuity	23
Gauss' Equation	24
Geometric Series	25
e^x	26
$\frac{dx}{dy}$	27
Intermediate Values	28
Mean Value	29

Taylor Series 30

The Squeeze Theorem 31

Strange Attractors 32

Turbulence 33

Fractals 34

Primes & Composites 37

GCD (a,b) = 1 38

Congruence 39

Phi(m) 40

Infinite Primes 41

Goldbach's Conjecture 42

Quadratic Residue 43

Infinite Descent 44

Sum of Two Squares 45

The Phi Function & the Sum of Divisors 46

Gaussian Integers 47

$\sqrt{p} \neq \frac{a}{b}$ 48

The Law of the Excluded Middle 49

Transcendentals 50

Pascal's Triangle 51

Mordell's Theorem 52

Heptadecagon 53

$\{\emptyset\}$ 57

∞ 58

Euler 59

Russell's Paradox 60

Sets 61

Sets $\rightarrow$ Groups 62

1 Identity 63

2 Inverse 64

3 Associativity 65

4 Closure 66

Complex 67

A Dialogue 68

$\div$ 0 69

Gödel 2 70

Gödel 1 71

Q: The Rational

POINT

We begin with definitions.
A language needs words
As a house needs a foundation.
A language of ideas needs well-defined things,
And not things, really,
But ideal things.

So it begins,
"A point is that which has no dimension"
An idea that is not a thing
Defined by its not-thingness.

A thing with no dimension
Neither breadth, nor width, nor length.
A location on a contour-less map.

Right here: this is a point.

DEFINITIONS & DIMENSIONS

A point has no length, no width, and no depth.
A point has no dimension.
A line has length, but no width and no depth.
A line has one dimension.
The intersection of two lines is a point.
Any two lines exist on a plane.
A plane has length and width, but no depth.
A plane has two dimensions.
The intersection of two planes is a line.
Any two planes exist in space.
Space has length, width, and depth.
Space has three dimensions.

The intersection of three-dimensional spaces is a plane.
And so on. . .

POSTULATE I

A thing needs an action,
A purpose.
A sentence is not a sentence without a verb.
There is no time without motion.

The first action is creation.
Create a point.
Give the point a name.

Now
Create a second point.
Give the point a name.

1. Between two points there is a line.

There is one and only one line.
It is born already named.
An act of creation ends
In a universal truth.

POSTULATE II

A line has only length.
Neither area, nor volume,
Nor space.
Only length.

If up and down,
Then never left or right.
If left and right,
Then never up or down.

Limited to one dimension
Yet infinite
Its length can always be increased.

2. A line can be extended.

POSTULATE III

A tree rises from the earth,
And the angle is right.
Water falls from great heights,
And the angle is right.
A tower reaches toward the sky,
And the angle is right.
A person holds their head high,
And the angle is right.

Two lines cross,
Four angles are created.
If those angles equal one another,
Then they are right.

3. All right angles are equal.

POSTULATE IV

4. A circle can be created
with
a point and a line.
A center and a radius
Allow a circle to exist.

Yet, the center is not a part
And the radius is not a part.
The circle is the points
A radius away
From the center.

The thing
Defined by its non-parts.
A location and a distance
Give a circle its being.
But a circle is not a location.
A circle is not a distance.

POSTULATE V

Two lines cross a third line.
On one side the two angles are less than a line:
Less than two right angles.
The lines will find each other.
What of the other side?

Two lines cross a third line.
On one side the two angles are greater than a line:
Greater than two right angles.
What of the other side?
The lines will find each other.

Two lines cross a third line.
On one side the two angles equal a line:
Equal two right angles.

Will the two lines find each other?
What of the other side?

5TH POSTULATE REVISITED

That the two lines never cross
Must be assumed.
Taken on faith.

It cannot be proved.

That it cannot be proved
Can be proved.

Can there be truth without proof?

AXIOM #1

I am the same as you
You are the same as me
If I am the same as them
They must the same as you
And you them.

This is the nature of equality.

AXIOMS #2 & 3

Things begin equal.
If they gain
The same
Or lose
The same
Equals remain equal

This is the basis for maintaining balance.

AXIOM #4

We are what we are
Neither more nor less.

A thing is equal
To its self.
How could it be otherwise?

AXIOM #5

The whole is greater
Than the part.
The branch needs the trunk for support.
The trunk needs the branch for sustenance.
The tree needs only the sun.

What is a leader without a pack?

TESSELATION

(Pythagoras)

A shape
Can be divided
Into triangles.
Which can be divided
Into right triangles.
Which are comprised of
Line segments
Which form the foundations
Of squares
The areas of which
Sum to one another.

Thus, the simplest shape
Provides the way
To all others.

PYTHAGOREAN TRIPLETS

Think of two numbers.

Square them and
Find the difference
Of the squares.
Call this A.

Multiply your two numbers
Double the product.
Call this B.

Square your two numbers.
Find the sum
Of the squares.
Call this C.

You have given birth to triplets.

3 PROBLEMS

1. Imagine a room.
All six sides are the same
Size and shape.
Double the room's size
While keeping its shape:
It cannot be done.

2. Imagine a slice of pie.
The crust makes an angle.
Share the pie evenly among three friends:
It cannot be done.

3. Imagine a puddle,
A circle,
made perfect by the rain.
Find a square that will hold the water
Perfectly:
It cannot be done.

Why are these things not possible?
Because they are not Rational.

A FAMOUS DEATH

A shadow fell on figures
In the dirt.

"Do not disturb my circles!"
The wise man demanded.

A blade fell.

R: The Real

THE FUNDAMENTAL THEOREM

A function tells you
Where
A thing can be found.

To derive a function is to ask
How
The thing is changing.

If you create an image
Of the change
The size of the image
Will show you
Where
The thing can be found.

Some questions lead to answers
That lead to questions
That return
To the source.

This truth is Fundamental.

LIMITS

We measure change
Between two points.
From here to there.
But not all paths are straight,
And something is lost.

Move the points closer together.
How close should they be?

As close as necessary.
Choose a distance
And I can build a bridge.
Narrow the distance
Until the bridge is no more
And nothing is lost.

CONTINUITY

Every point has a role.
The road we take
Is paved by the all.
Each point a stepping-stone
on our road.

As we approach each stone
From either direction
We find a foundation
At each step,
And we never lose our footing.

This is called continuity.

GAUSS' EQUATION

Take a list,
And combine its parts.

What do you get?

Step back.
Find the patterns.

Be like the child.

Start on the outside
And work toward the center.

GEOMETRIC SERIES

Some will collapse
While others rise
To the infinite.

It is not where we begin
That decides our end.
But rather,
How we grow.

$$e^X$$

Curves change.
If they did not change,
They would not be curves.

One curve's change
Is equal to its position.
Its direction is its velocity.

Moving at the speed
Of its self.
Like a person who can accept who they are
Right now.

$$\frac{dx}{dy}$$

Things may change their position,
But their place can be found.

Things may change their speed
Between their positions,
And their speed can be found.

Things may change their acceleration
Between their speeds,
And their acceleration can be found.

Look closer,
When the between becomes
Infinitely small
Your sight becomes infinite.

INTERMEDIATE VALUES

Life begins.
Life ends.

In between
The beginning and the end
There are highs
There are lows

And there is every point
In between.

MEAN VALUE

Life has ups and downs.
There are fast times and slow times.
Find the center.

It exists,
Because it must.

TAYLOR SERIES

Take something that is
Infinitely complex
And consider its source.
Understand its behavior
At its beginning.

Consider the behavior of something that is
Infinitely complex.
Consider the behavior at its source.
Understand the behavior of
The behavior
At its beginning.

And so on. . .

Sometimes a thing is equal to
The sum of its parts
Even if its parts
Are infinite.

THE SQUEEZE THEOREM

You may know your limits.
The top and the bottom.

Realize they are the same
And you will find yourself.

STRANGE ATTRACTORS

Perhaps
If there was only one
It could rest.

Perhaps
Even two could come together
And find stability:
Stasis.
But there are more,
Always more.
And so change
Is the only constant.

And while one may be drawn
To another.
Many will wander
And create patterns
With their wanderings

You may guess at the flow
Of their wanderings,
But do not pretend
That you know
Where their journey leads them.

TURBULENCE

The boundaries
Of order and disorder
Provide a glimpse

Into cycles
That repeat themselves
Without ever
Retracing their steps.

Following infinite paths
All moving in the same direction
But never the same.

Fluctuations arise,
Subtle ripples
Expand and repeat
To create
Horrendous storms.

FRACTALS

Look.

Look at life.
At the patterns that allow
Life to flourish.
The leaf resembles the tree
The tree resembles the forest.

Look.

Look at the land.
At the patterns that arise
The sand resembles the beach.
The beach resembles the coast.

Look closer
You will see.

Step back
You will see.

N: The Natural

PRIMES & COMPOSITES

Each is comprised of its unique parts.

The whole is always present.
Unity is always present.
All things are a product of unity and the self.

Those that are only a product
Of unity and the self
Are said to be Prime.

All others are composed
Of primes.

Primality is the foundation.

GCD $(a,b) = 1$

When two things exist
Having nothing in common
They share unity.
And their products share their all.

A base of one
Can lead down a path
That is infinite.

CONGRUENCE

If a thing is a part
Of our difference,

Then we are the same
In the eyes of this thing,
This part
Of our difference.

If we should increase or decrease
Together,
Our difference remains the same.

Linked by our difference
We share congruence.

PHI(m)

Count all of the things
that you are not.
This is your phi.

The number of your non-qualities.

If you are a product of primes
Then your phi is a product
Of their non-qualities.

What you lack
Combining
To define you.

INFINITE PRIMES

"Infinity plus 1!"
A child yells, competitively.
The child understands:
Infinity needs a rule
That allows it to grow.

There is always a bigger number
Because there is always a plus 1.

Can we count the Primes?

Multiply them all
And plus 1.

Now divide.

GOLDBACH'S CONJECTURE

All even numbers
Are the sum of two primes
Unless they are not.

Every prime number
Up to 200,000,000,000
Is the sum of two primes.

Do 200,000,000,000 examples make a thing true?

No.

QUADRATIC RESIDUE

A cyclical system,
Like a spinning wheel,
Always provides another
opportunity.

Sometimes,
When there seems to be nothing
In common
Rising to a higher power
offers another opportunity,

And reveals a solution.

INFINITE DESCENT

Assume that *it* is.
And Reduce it
to its source.

What brought about the source?

Reduce this to its source.
And so on. . .
Infinitely

You see?
The assumption was wrong.
How can *it* be?
If it is balancing on a pillar
With no bottom?

SUM OF TWO SQUARES

Sometimes a path can lead to the unexpected.
Seeking the sums
Of numbers squared
Reveals a connection
To the remainders
Of numbers quartered.

Look closely
And you find a list of triplets.

THE PHI FUNCTION & THE
SUM OF DIVISORS

All that is
Contains
All that is not.

There is no light
Without darkness.
There is no sound
Without silence.

Every product that is Whole
Contains factors.
Look closely at all that they are not.

The sum of the non-factors
Will equal the Whole.

GAUSSIAN INTEGERS

A master once lived
In the world that is Real;
A master who could predict the cosmos.
Knowing where to find
Things that could not be seen.

The master could see
Every branch on the tree.
He revolutionized all of the known branches
And many that were not yet known.

Having tamed that which was Real
The master turned his eyes
To the Imaginary.

The master found many connections
And uncovered many truths.
Proving, among other things,
That the Imaginary too
could be tamed.

$$\sqrt{p} \neq \frac{a}{b}$$

Consider,
The root of a prime
Cannot be Rational.

Rationality implies a ratio.
A ratio is a relationship between two parts.

If there were such a ratio
Then one of its parts
Would be a part of a prime.

But primes have no parts,
So the root cannot be Rational.

A contradiction sometimes leads
To a truth.

THE LAW OF THE EXCLUDED MIDDLE

A statement can either be true
Or it can be false.

Can a statement be neither?
Can it be both?

TRANSCENDENTALS

Imagine, if you will,
A line of numbers:
Numbers that can be as large as you like.
Or as small.

Between any two numbers
There is a line of numbers.
A line as long as you like.
Even if the two numbers are closer
Than you can imagine.

No matter how small the distance
Between two numbers
There is always a line:
Countable, though you could never count it.

And yet,
There are gaps in the line.
Numbers that will not be found.
There are so many numbers missing,
That they are uncountable.

Our line is infinitely dense
And yet,
There are so many gaps that our line
Can hardly be said to exist at all.

PASCAL'S TRIANGLE

$$1$$
$$1\ 1$$
$$1\ 2\ 1$$
$$1\ 3\ 3\ 1$$
$$1\ 4\ 6\ 4\ 1$$
$$1\ 5\ 10\ 10\ 5\ 1$$
$$1\ 6\ 15\ 20\ 15\ 6\ 1$$
$$1\ 7\ 21\ 35\ 35\ 21\ 7\ 1$$

And so on. . .

MORDELL'S THEOREM

To find the Rational
In so much complexity,
Focus on what is known.

One answer can lead to another.
Two answers can lead to a third.

Reflect on the known
To find its opposite.

Sometimes a straight line
Can predict where a curved path will lead.

HEPTADECAGON

Simplify the problem.

Narrow the scope to
One measurement.
Can you find this measurement?
Can this measurement be found?

This leads you down a path
Past imaginary plots
And into nested problems.

Problems within problems.

The path ends in a solution
Hidden on ancient texts
Speaking of a type of number.
A type that may be infinite,

Or maybe there are only five.

C: The Complex

{Ø}

In the beginning there was nothing.
Then there was the word: nothing.
And the word was a thing.
And "thing" was a word.
So there were two things.

If there are two things, then there must be three.
And so on. . .

∞

Where does it end?
All things end,

Except number.

This is the source of power.
Math gives not-ending its name.
But the name is not the thing,
The idea is the thing.
The idea allows us to approach the truth.

With infinity we achieve perfection.

EULER

The one-eyed man designed a ship
Though he had never seen the sea.
The ship was beautiful, his calculations pristine.
He was given second place.
The ship was impractical, unrealistic.

"If reality and my numbers are in dispute,"
The one-eyed man responded,
"Then it is reality that is to be blamed."

RUSSELL'S PARADOX

There is a thing
A container of sorts
That contains all the things
That do not contain themselves.

Does this thing contain itself?

SETS

The excited child returns home,
"Look, I have a new toy!"
The confused parent sees nothing.
"It is a set of nothing,
an empty set."

The child puts the empty set with their other toys.
The set of toys already had an empty set.
But children do not know such things.

The parent does not see the value
In the empty set.
Adults do not know such things.

What is larger,
The set of all sets
Or the set of all things?

SETS → GROUPS

A collection of family members
A collection of toys
A collection of ideas
A collection of numbers

The mind seeks connections
Any collection is possible
This is called the Theory of Sets.

A set exists without action.
It simply is.
But a sentence needs both a noun and a verb.

A set whose elements share a common action
Is called a group.

1
IDENTITY

One member must reflect each of the others
So that each sees itself
In the Identity.

And in the Identity
Each sees itself.

It is an essential non-effect
Each element returns to itself.

2
INVERSE

Equal and Opposite
They return to the source.
Hot and Cold
Light and Dark
Positive and Negative
Only together
Do they find an
Identity.

3
ASSOCIATIVITY

Outside of time
There is no cause.
There is no effect.
All action simply is.

No one is first
When order does not matter.

4
CLOSURE

Fish combine to make more fish.
Deer combine to make more deer.
Ice becomes water becomes vapor.
What is ice?
What is water?
What is vapor?

This is called closure.

COMPLEX

To find the area from the length
Is simple
And Rational.

To find the length from the area
Is more difficult,
And connects to what is Real.

Imagine an area that is negative
To grasp the root of the complex.

A DIALOGUE

Q: What can be accomplished with the Naturals?
A: Actions of growth:
addition, multiplication, and exponential powers.

Q: What can be accomplished with the Integers?
A: All of the above can be accomplished with the Integers,
And subtraction as well.

Q: What can be accomplished with the Rationals?
A: All of the above can be accomplished with the Rationals,
And division as well.
Except for zero, that alone cannot be divided.

Q: What can be accomplished with the Reals?
A: All of the above can be accomplished with the Reals,
And all positive roots as well.

Q: What can be accomplished with the Complex?
A: With the Complex all actions are possible
Except division by zero.

This can never be done.
It is our one prohibition.

$\div\ 0$

Zero does not divide any number.
Thus, nothing can be divided by zero.
To try is to chase infinity,
But infinity is not a destination.

A dialogue:
Science has shown that the Universe is expanding.
True.
How can the universe be infinite if it is expanding?
How could the Universe be Infinite if it was not?

GÖDEL 2

If one does not lie
Then there are things
That one cannot say.

How can one be sure
That one does not lie?
One must look outside
One's self.

But in looking outside
One creates the possibility
Of trusting one who lies.

Anything can be said
By a liar.
If there are things
That one cannot say
Does this imply
That one does not lie?

GÖDEL 1

Not all thoughts
Can be spoken

There are facts
That cannot be proved

How do I know
Some facts cannot be proved?

A fact told me,
"I am unprovable."
And yet it remained
A Fact.

Made in the USA
Las Vegas, NV
27 August 2021